Big!

By Daisy Hawkins

shed in 2026 by
wood House Press
4 Clinton Street
lo, NY 14224

ed in the United States of America

Library of Congress Cataloging-in-Publication Data:
Names: Hawkins, Daisy, author. | Pinelli, Amerigo, illustrator.
Title: Big! / written by Daisy Hawkins. The Pips / written by Daisy Hawkins, illustrated by Amerigo Pinelli.
Description: Buffalo, NY : Norwood House Press, 2026. | Series: Phonics all-stars: phase 3 |
Identifiers: ISBN 9781978577930 (pbk.) | ISBN 9781978577947 (library bound) | ISBN 9781978577954 (ebook)
Subjects: LCSH: Reading–Phonetic method–Juvenile literature. | English language–Phonetics–Juvenile literature. | Bands (Music)–Juvenile literature. | Musicians–Juvenile literature.
Classification: LCC LB1573.3 H395 2026 | DDC 372.465–dc23

CPSIA compliance information: Batch #CW26NHP: For further information contact Norwood House Press at 1-800-237-9932.

Can Kaz rap?

Yes, Kaz can rap.

Can Yaffa pen Kaz a hit?

Yes, Yaffa can pen Kaz a hit.

Can Zen get a top mix?

Yes, Zen can get a top mix.

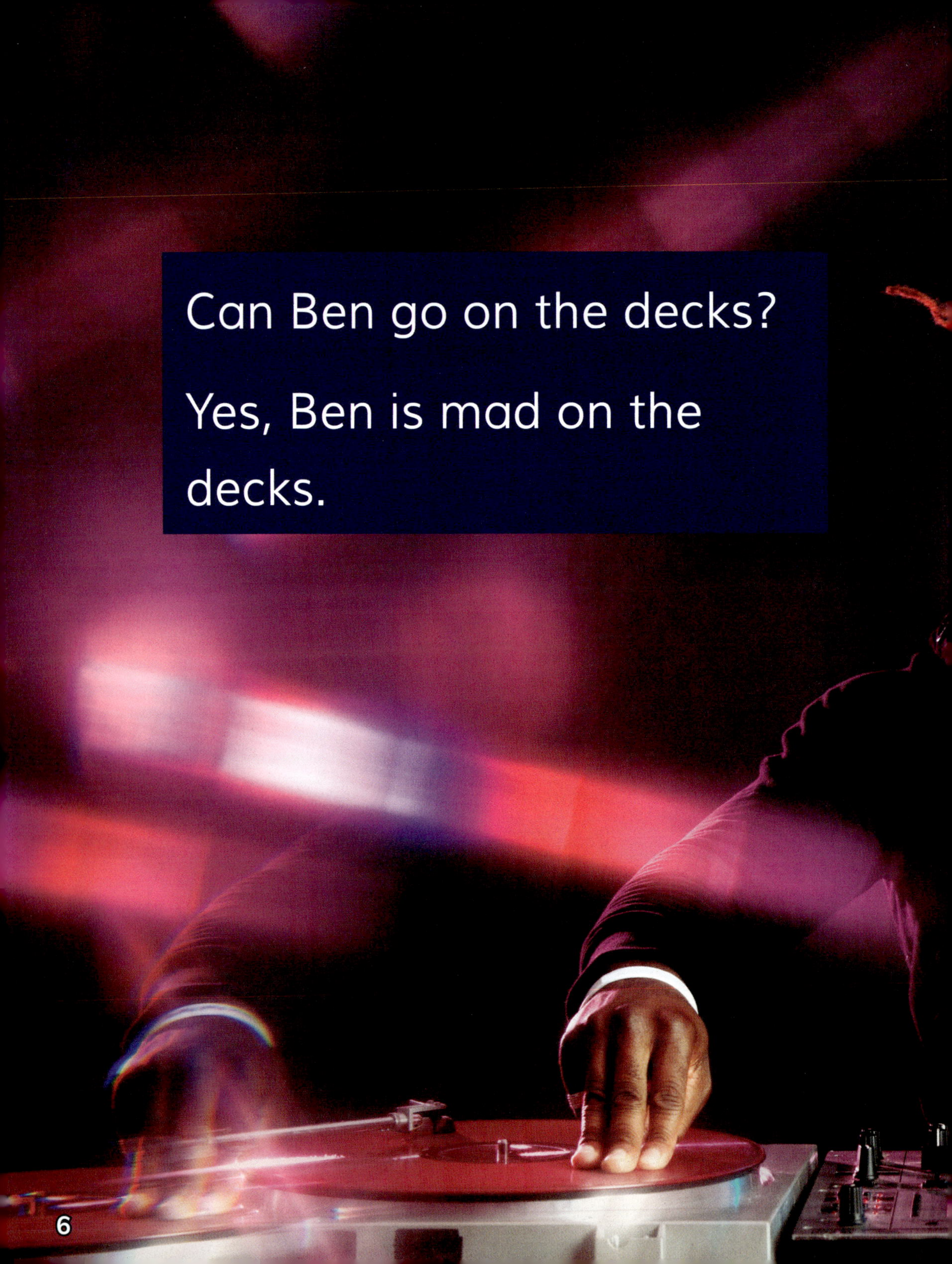

Can Ben go on the decks?

Yes, Ben is mad on the decks.

PRO MIXER DJ

PRO SHOW
WWW.PROSHOW.BY
NO. 005
ПЛОЩАДКА
14

If we get a gig, can Jack get the gear to the gig?

Yes, Jack can get it to the gig.

And me?

I can sell it.

I can sell pop, hip hop, rock, or jazz.

We will get into the top ten.
We will be **big!**

The Pips

Written by
Daisy Hawkins

Illustrated by
Amerigo Pinelli

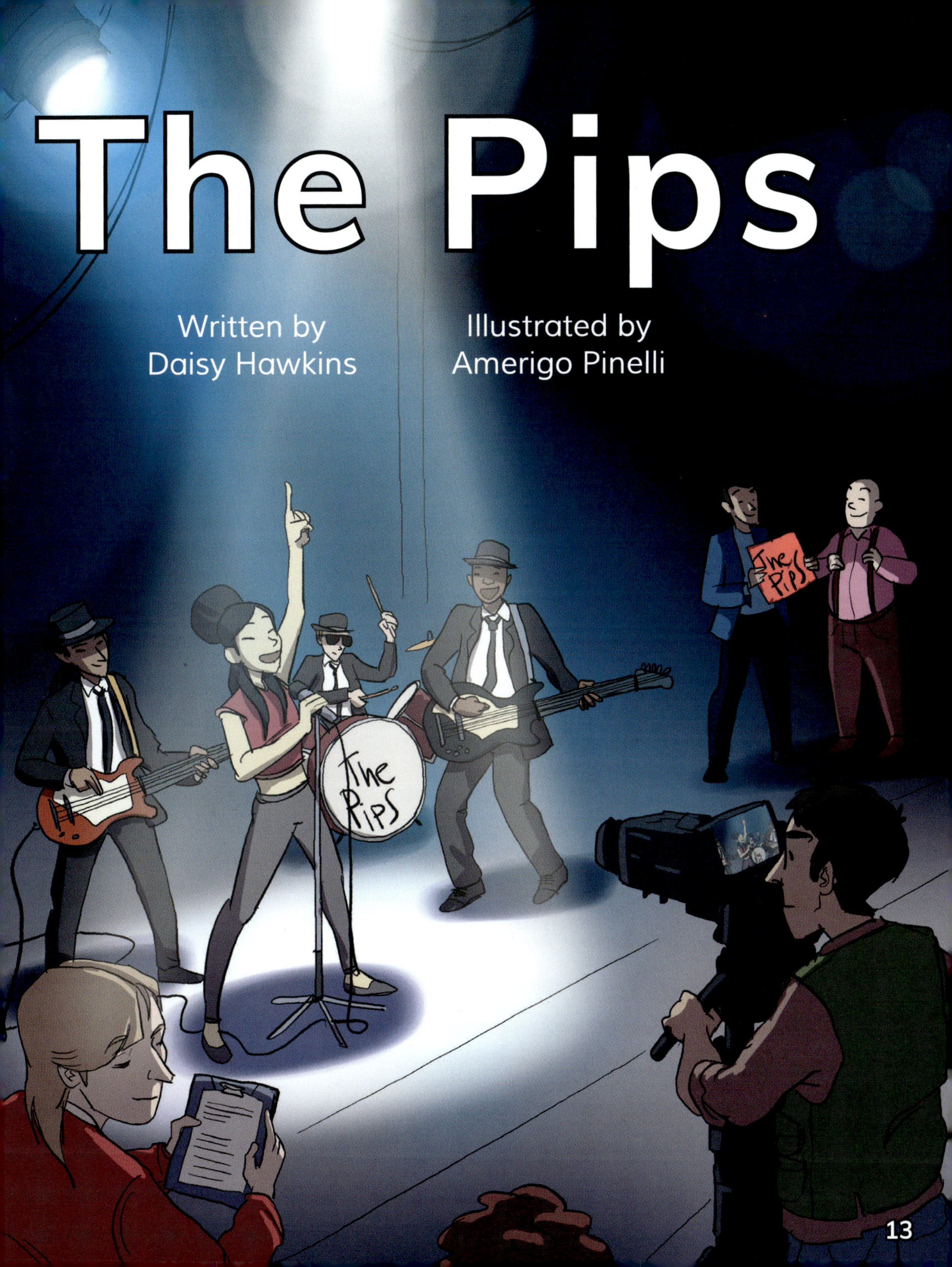

Zan is the best.

Will Zan get a job?

Zan gets a job.
It is not jazz – it is pop.

It is **Zan and The Pips.**

We will go to the top. We will be the fans' pick.

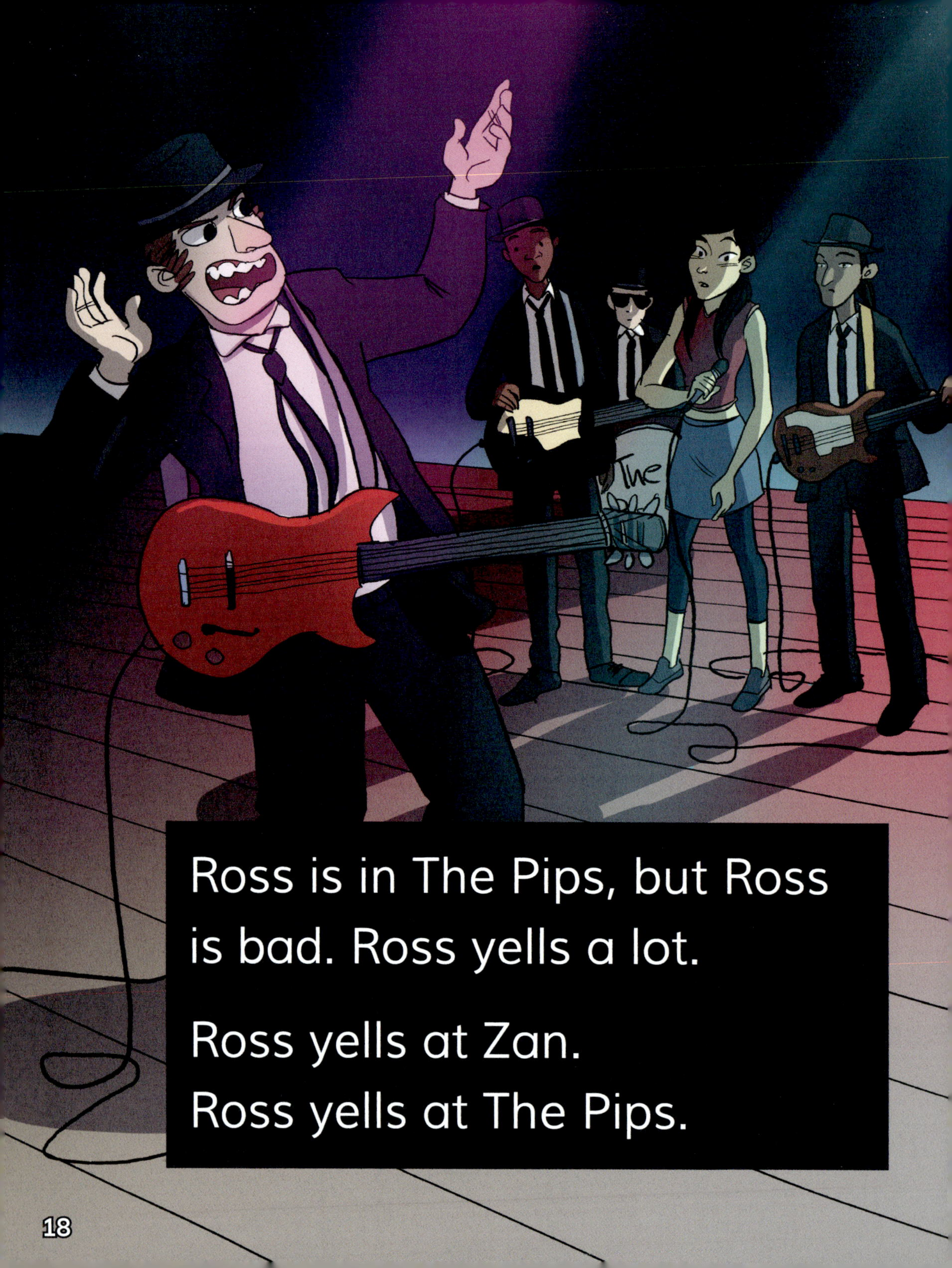

Ross is in The Pips, but Ross is bad. Ross yells a lot.

Ross yells at Zan.
Ross yells at The Pips.

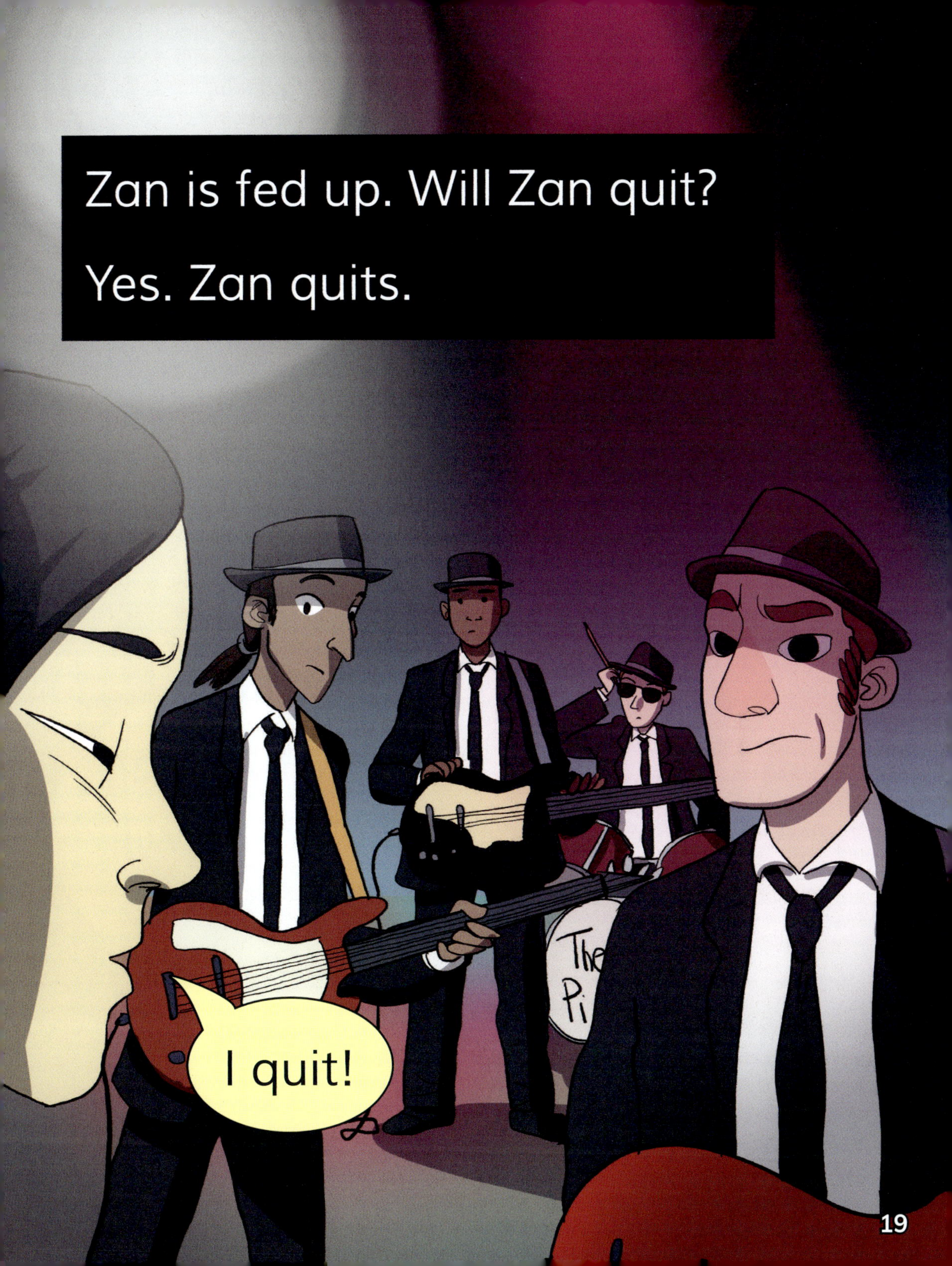
Zan is fed up. Will Zan quit?
Yes. Zan quits.
I quit!

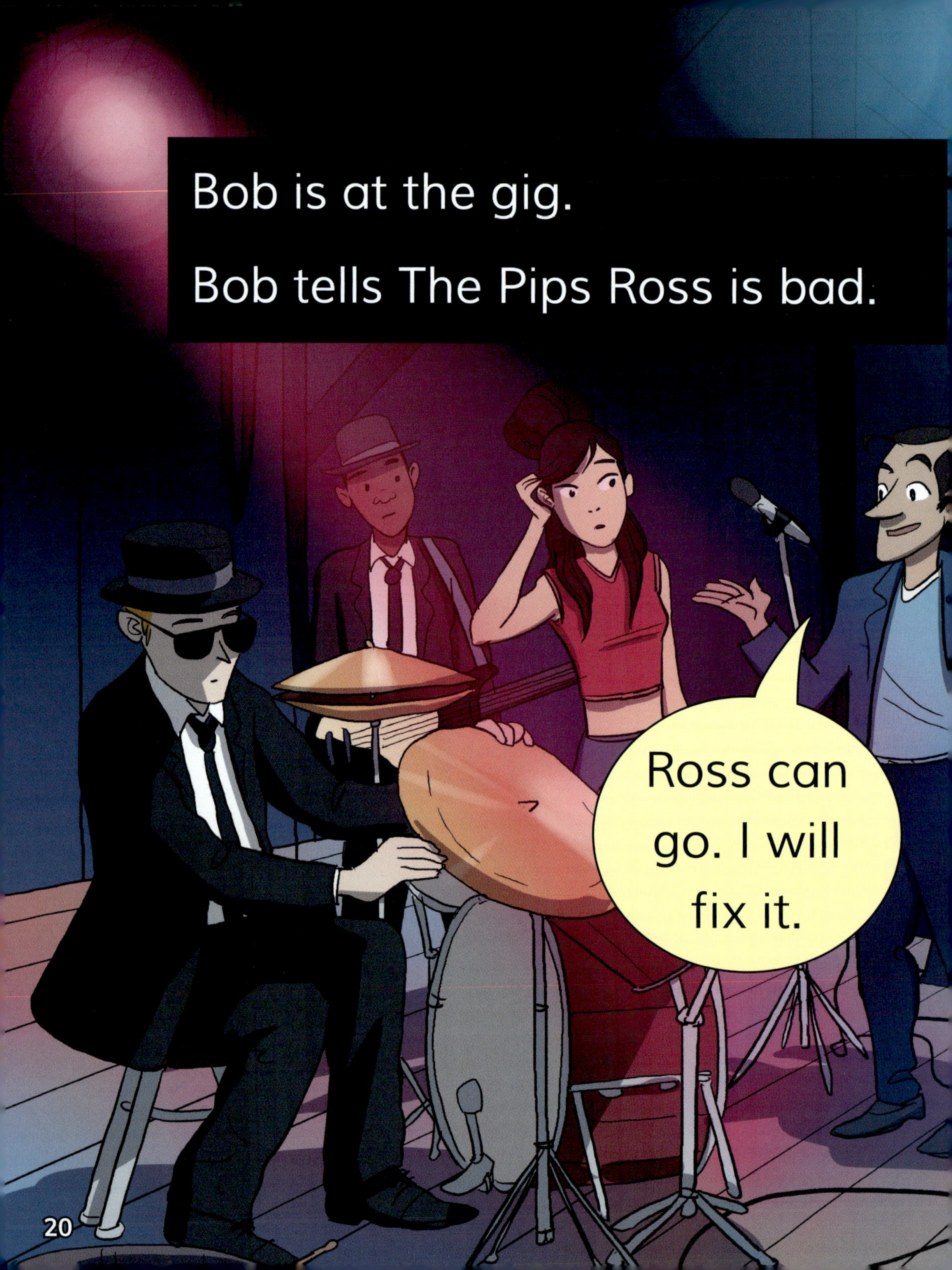
Bob is at the gig.
Bob tells The Pips Ross is bad.
Ross can go. I will fix it.

But Zan is the best. I am into **Zan and The Pips.**

The Pips will not back Ross.
Ross has to go.

Ross gets the sack.

Zan did not quit.

Zan picks The Pips.

Bob gets **Zan and The Pips** into the top ten.
It is a quick pop hit.
The Pips